D0049282

YOU
ARE SO
AWESOME.

summersdale

YOU ARE SO AWESOME

Summersdale Publishers Ltd
46 West Street
Chichester
West Sussex
PO19 1RP
UK

www.summersdale.com

Printed and bound in the Czech Republic

ISBN: 978-1-84953-958-6

Substantial discounts on bulk quantities of Summersdale books are available to corporations, professional associations and other organisations. For details contact general enquiries: telephone: +44 (0) 1243 771107 or email: enquiries@summersdale.com.

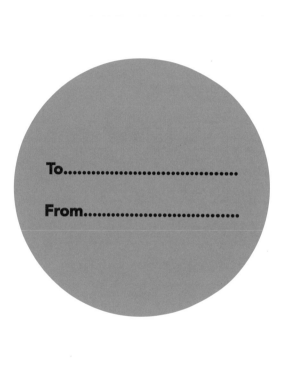

To...

From.....................................

Believe you can
and you're
halfway there.

Theodore Roosevelt

Success is getting what you want; happiness is wanting what you get.

W. P. Kinsella

Every strike brings
me closer to the
next home run.

Babe Ruth

THINK BIG AND DON'T LISTEN TO PEOPLE WHO TELL YOU IT CAN'T BE DONE. LIFE'S TOO SHORT TO THINK SMALL.

Tim Ferriss

Don't waste your energy trying to change opinions... do your thing, and don't care if they like it.

Tina Fey

As soon as you trust
yourself, you will
know how to live.

Johann Wolfgang von Goethe

It is confidence in our bodies, minds and spirits that allows us to keep looking for new adventures.

Oprah Winfrey

Successful people have fear, successful people have doubts, and successful people have worries. They don't let these feelings stop them.

T. Harv Eker

GOOD THINGS ARE GOING TO HAPPEN!

Tension is who you
think you should be;
relaxation is who you are.

Chinese proverb

Never dull your shine
for anybody else.

Tyra Banks

OTHER PEOPLE'S OPINION OF YOU DOES NOT HAVE TO BECOME YOUR REALITY.

Les Brown

Just as much as we see in others we have in ourselves.

William Hazlitt

A person can grow only as much as his horizon allows.

John Powell

Dare to be honest
and fear no labour.

Robert Burns

THE POWER OF A BOLD IDEA UTTERED PUBLICLY IN DEFIANCE OF DOMINANT OPINION CANNOT BE EASILY MEASURED.

Howard Zinn

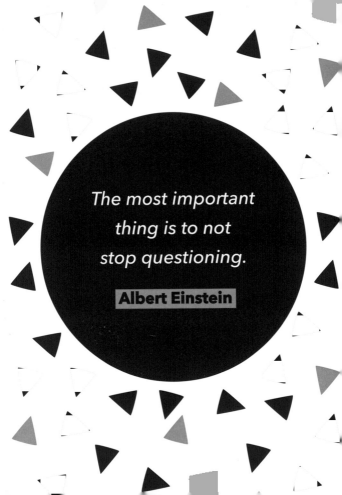

The most important thing is to not stop questioning.

Albert Einstein

WHEREVER YOU GO, GO WITH ALL YOUR HEART.

Confucius

POSITIVE MIND

POSITIVE VIBES

POSITIVE
LIFE.

The shell must break
before the bird must fly.

Alfred, Lord Tennyson

Your work is to discover
your world and then
with all your heart
give yourself to it.

Buddha

**Rise above
the storm and
you will find
sunshine.**

Mario Fernandez

He who has a 'why' to live for
can bear almost any 'how'.

Friedrich Nietzsche

I'VE GOT A THEORY THAT IF YOU GIVE 100 PERCENT ALL OF THE TIME, SOMEHOW THINGS WILL WORK OUT IN THE END.

Larry Bird

I can be changed by what happens to me. But I refuse to be reduced by it.

Maya Angelou

TRUST YOURSELF; BELIEVE THAT YOU HAVE A UNIQUE DESTINY TO FULFIL.

Candy Paull

Big shots are only little shots who keep shooting.

Christopher Morley

You must think well
of yourself. You must
see yourself as worth
celebrating, worth
loving, worth having.

Angelina Talpa

No one except you alone
can change your life.

M. K. Soni

CELEBRATE
EVERY
VICTORY.

You cannot change what
you are, only what you do.

Philip Pullman

Act as if what
you do makes a
difference. It does.

William James

ALWAYS BE A FIRST-RATE VERSION OF YOURSELF AND NOT A SECOND-RATE VERSION OF SOMEONE ELSE.

Judy Garland

Do what you can,
with what you have,
where you are.

Theodore Roosevelt

Follow your
own star.

Dante Alighieri

**JUST DON'T
GIVE UP TRYING
TO DO WHAT
YOU REALLY
WANT TO DO.**

Ella Fitzgerald

Everyone has been
made for some particular
work, and the desire
for that work has been
put in every heart.

Rumi

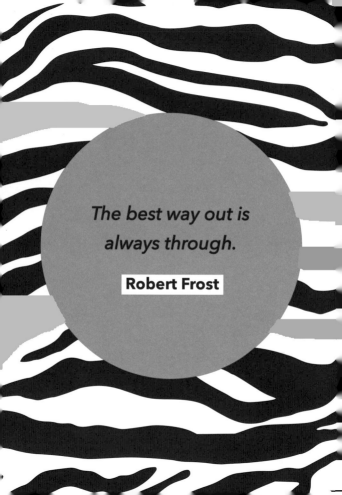

The best way out is always through.

Robert Frost

Take the first step in faith. You don't have to see the whole staircase, just take the first step.

Martin Luther King Jr

Attitudes are contagious – make yours worth catching.

Anonymous

NEVER REGRET SOMETHING THAT ONCE MADE YOU SMILE.

Amber Deckers

BELIEVE YOU CAN AND YOU WILL!

The moment you doubt
whether you can fly,
you cease forever to
be able to do it.

J. M. Barrie

ARDENTLY DO
TODAY WHAT
MUST BE DONE.

Buddha

Trust yourself. You know more than you think you do.

Benjamin Spock

Anything is possible
once you believe you are
worthy of achieving it.

Jason Pockrandt

Be yourself; everyone else is taken.

Anonymous

Light tomorrow
with today.

Elizabeth Barrett Browning

NOTHING CAN DIM THE LIGHT THAT SHINES FROM WITHIN.

Maya Angelou

When you discover something that nourishes your soul, care enough about yourself to make room for it in your life.

Jean Shinoda Bolen

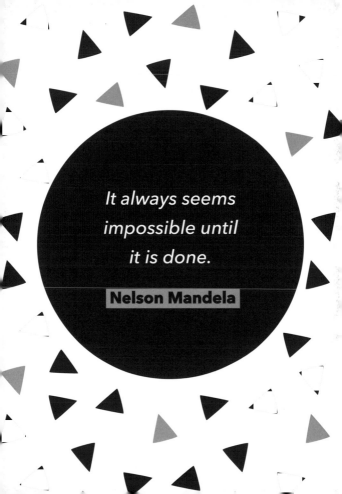

THOSE WHO DON'T BELIEVE IN MAGIC...

WILL NEVER
FIND IT.

A man cannot be comfortable without his own approval.

Mark Twain

Once you choose hope
anything is possible.

Christopher Reeve

Our greatest glory is not in never failing, but in rising up every time we fail.

Confucius

Life is like riding a bicycle.
To keep your balance
you must keep moving.

Albert Einstein

Nurture your mind with great thoughts. To believe in the heroic makes heroes.

Benjamin Disraeli

THE DREAMERS ARE THE SAVIOURS OF THE WORLD.

James Allen

The first step is to say that you can.

Will Smith

BE A VOICE
NOT AN ECHO.

Anonymous

I do not believe in taking the right decision. I take a decision and make it right.

Muhammad Ali Jinnah

Believe that life is worth living and your belief will help create the fact.

William James

BE GENTLE WITH YOURSELF.

What lies behind us and what lies before us are tiny matters compared to what lies within us.

Ralph Waldo Emerson

The true nobility is in being superior to your previous self.

Hindu proverb

YOU ARE VERY POWERFUL, PROVIDED YOU KNOW HOW POWERFUL YOU ARE.

Yogi Bhajan

The person who says it cannot be done should not interrupt the person who is doing it.

Chinese proverb

Unfold your own myth.

Rumi

DO ANYTHING, BUT LET IT PRODUCE JOY.

Walt Whitman

It doesn't matter where you are coming from. All that matters is where you are going.

Brian Tracy

Dreaming, after all, is
a form of planning.

Gloria Steinhem

WE BECOME WHAT
WE THINK ABOUT.

Earl Nightingale

TO ESTABLISH TRUE SELF-ESTEEM WE MUST CONCENTRATE ON OUR SUCCESSES.

Denis Waitley

Be faithful to that which exists nowhere but in yourself.

André Gide

EVERY DAY IS A FRESH START.

Who looks outside, dreams;
who looks inside, awakes.

Carl Jung

Believe in your flyness and conquer your shyness.

Kanye West

**CLIMB FROM
THE DEPTHS OF
YOUR SOUL TO
THE HEIGHTS OF
YOUR FUTURE.**

Terri Guillemets

Be not afraid of greatness;
some are born great,
some achieve greatness,
and others have greatness
thrust upon 'em.'

William Shakespeare

The best way to predict the future is to invent it.

Alan Kay

Always be yourself… do not go out and look for a successful personality and try to duplicate it.

Bruce Lee

PRIDE IS HOLDING YOUR HEAD UP WHEN EVERYONE AROUND YOU HAS THEIRS BOWED. COURAGE IS WHAT MAKES YOU DO IT.

Bryce Courtenay

Creativity means believing you have greatness.

Wayne Dyer

Once we believe in
ourselves, we can
risk curiosity, wonder,
spontaneous delight,
or any experience that
reveals the human spirit.

E. E. Cummings

DON'T
COUNT
THE DAYS...

MAKE
THE DAYS
COUNT.

You wouldn't worry so much about what others think of you if you realised how seldom they do.

Eleanor Roosevelt

TALK TO YOURSELF LIKE YOU WOULD TO SOMEONE YOU LOVE.

Brené Brown

Man is only truly great when he acts from his passions.

Benjamin Disraeli

The key to life is accepting challenges.

Bette Davis

The way to develop self-confidence is to do the thing you fear and get successful experiences behind you.

William Jennings Bryan

Life is ten per cent what
you experience and
ninety per cent how
you respond to it.

Dorothy M. Neddermeyer

*I do not care so much
what I am to others as I care
what I am to myself.*

Michel de Montaigne

To be yourself in a world that is constantly trying to make you something else is the greatest complishment.

Ralph Waldo Emerson

If any man seeks
greatness, let him
forget greatness and
ask for truth, and
he will find both.

Horace Mann

OPTIMISM IS THE FAITH THAT LEADS TO ACHIEVEMENT. NOTHING CAN BE DONE WITHOUT HOPE AND CONFIDENCE.

Helen Keller

BE ORIGINAL.

If you compare yourself with others, you'll become vain; for always there will be greater and lesser persons than yourself.

Max Ehrmann

You are magnificent
beyond measure, perfect
in your imperfections,
and wonderfully made.

Abiola Abrams

If you're presenting yourself with confidence, you can pull off pretty much anything.

Katy Perry

Reflect upon your present blessings, of which every man has many – not on your past misfortunes, of which all men have some.

Charles Dickens

Put your future in good hands: your own.

Anonymous

If you hear a voice within you that says, 'You cannot paint,' then by all means paint, and the voice will be silenced.

Vincent van Gogh

IF WE DID ALL THE THINGS WE ARE CAPABLE OF DOING, WE WOULD LITERALLY ASTOUND OURSELVES.

Thomas Edison

KNOCK THE 'T' OFF THE 'CAN'T'.

Anonymous

Start by doing what's
necessary; then
what's possible; and
suddenly you're doing
the impossible.

St Francis of Assisi

To know how to do something well is to enjoy it.

Pearl S. Buck

ONE PART AT
A TIME, ONE
DAY AT A
TIME, WE CAN
ACCOMPLISH
ANY GOAL
WE SET FOR
OURSELVES.

Karen Casey

YOU ARE CAPABLE OF AMAZING THINGS.

Always hold your head up, but be careful to keep your nose at a friendly level.

Max L. Forman

Do not doubt the goodness in you.

Dodinsky

CHIEFLY THE MOULD OF MAN'S FORTUNE IS IN HIS OWN HANDS.

Francis Bacon

If you are going to doubt something, doubt your limits.

Don Ward

Opportunity doesn't knock; it presents itself when you beat down the door.

Kyle Chandler

SUCCESS IS THE SMALL SUM OF EFFORTS – REPEATED DAY IN AND DAY OUT.

Robert Collier

A great figure or physique is nice, but it's self-confidence that makes someone really sexy.

Vivica A. Fox

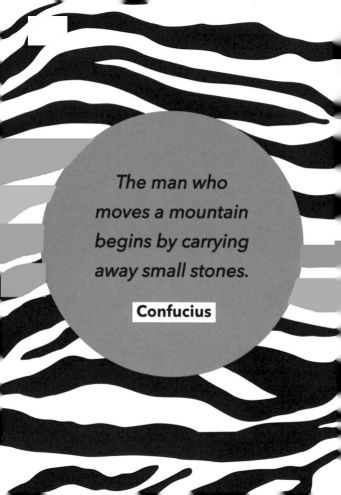

The man who moves a mountain begins by carrying away small stones.

Confucius

You need to believe in yourself and what you do. Be tenacious and genuine.

Christian Louboutin

DON'T
WAIT FOR
OPPORTUNITY.

CREATE IT.

Be unapologetically you.

Steve Mariboli

THE MORE WE DO, THE MORE WE CAN DO.

William Hazlitt

Follow your inner moonlight; don't hide the madness.

Allen Ginsberg

We are more than
what we do, much
more than what we
accomplish, far more
than what we possess.

William Arthur Ward

THE GREATEST DOER MUST ALSO BE THE GREATEST DREAMER.

Theodore Roosevelt

I cannot do everything, but still I can do something. And because I cannot do everything I will not refuse to do the something that I can do.

Edward Everett Hale

The question isn't who is going to let me; it's who is going to stop me.

Ayn Rand

*We don't know
who we are until we
see what we can do.*

Martha Grimes

WE ARE WHAT WE REPEATEDLY DO. EXCELLENCE IS THEREFORE NOT AN ACT BUT A HABIT.

Aristotle

I am not afraid of storms
for I am learning how
to sail my ship.

Louisa May Alcott

BE THE BEST YOU CAN BE.

We don't see things
as they are; we see
them as we are.

Anaïs Nin

Love yourself first
and everything else
falls into line.

Lucille Ball

DON'T ASK YOURSELF WHAT THE WORLD NEEDS. ASK YOURSELF WHAT MAKES YOU COME ALIVE, AND THEN GO AND DO THAT.

Howard Thurman

The reward for conformity
is that everyone likes
you but yourself.

Rita Mae Brown

Do not let what you cannot do interfere with what you can do.

John Wooden

Whether you think you can or think you can't – you are right.

Henry Ford

Take time to deliberate; but when the time for action arrives, stop thinking and go in.

Napoleon Bonaparte

Those who wish to sing always find a song.

Swedish proverb

PEARLS DON'T LIE ON THE SEASHORE. IF YOU WANT ONE, YOU MUST DIVE FOR IT.

Chinese proverb

A clear vision, backed by definite plans, gives you a tremendous feeling of confidence and personal power.

Brian Tracy

Dreams are free,
so free your dreams.

Terri Guillemets

START EACH DAY WITH A POSITIVE THOUGHT.

Always go with your
passions. Never
ask yourself if it's
realistic or not.

Deepak Chopra

Go out on a limb. That's where the fruit is.

Jimmy Carter

ONE IMPORTANT KEY TO SUCCESS IS SELF-CONFIDENCE. AN IMPORTANT KEY TO SELF-CONFIDENCE IS PREPARATION.

Arthur Ashe

Each one of us should
lead a life stirring enough
to start a movement.

Max Lucado

Don't quit. Suffer now and live the rest of your life as a champion.

Muhammad Ali

How often in life we
complete a task that was
beyond the capability
of the person we were
when we first started it.

Robert Brault

ALL OUR DREAMS CAN COME TRUE IF WE HAVE THE COURAGE TO PURSUE THEM.

Walt Disney

IT AIN'T WHAT THEY CALL YOU, IT'S WHAT YOU ANSWER TO.

W. C. Fields

Life shrinks or expands
in proportion to
one's courage.

Anaïs Nin

TAKE
TIME TO
DO WHAT